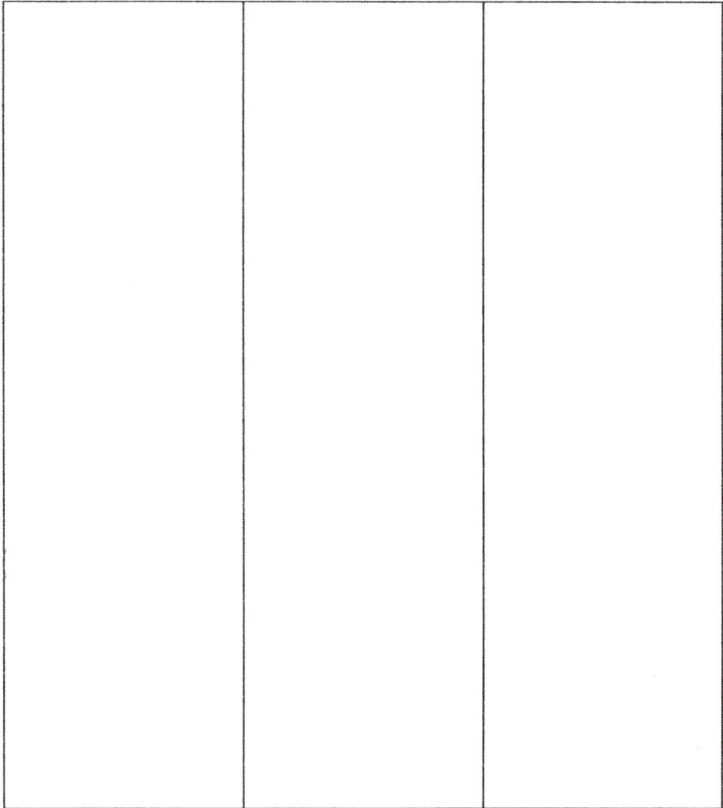

This book is on loan from Library Services for Schools

Westmorland
& Furness
Council

Cumberland
Council

Working for **Cumberland Council** and
Westmorland & Furness Council

First published in Great Britain 2024 by Farshore
An imprint of HarperCollins*Publishers*
1 London Bridge Street, London SE1 9GF
www.farshore.co.uk

HarperCollins*Publishers*
Macken House, 39/40 Mayor Street Upper,
Dublin 1, D01 C9W8, Ireland

Written by Tom Stone
Illustrations by Joe McLaren
Special thanks to Sherin Kwan, Alex Wiltshire, Jay Castello,
Kelsey Ranallo, Lauren Marklund and Milo Bengtsson

This book is an original creation by Farshore

MOJANG
S T U D I O S

ISBN 978 0 00 861561 1
Printed in UK
1

ONLINE SAFETY FOR YOUNGER FANS

Spending time online is great fun! Here are a few simple rules to help younger fans stay safe and
keep the internet a great place to spend time:
- Never give out your real name – don't use it as your username.
- Never give out any of your personal details.
- Never tell anybody which school you go to or how old you are.
- Never tell anybody your password except a parent or a guardian.
- Be aware that you must be 13 or over to create an account on many sites.
Always check the site policy and ask a parent or guardian for permission before registering.
- Always tell a parent or guardian if something is worrying you.
Stay safe online. Any website addresses listed in this book are correct at the time of going to print.
However, Farshore is not responsible for content hosted by third parties. Please be aware that online
content can be subject to change and websites can contain content that is unsuitable for children.
We advise that all children are supervised when using the internet.

Stay safe online. Farshore is not responsible for content hosted by third parties.

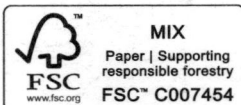

MIX
Paper | Supporting
responsible forestry
FSC™ C007454

This book contains FSC™ certified paper and other controlled
sources to ensure responsible forest management.

For more information visit: www.harpercollins.co.uk/green

MINECRAFT

TIPS, TRICKS & HACKS

CONTENTS

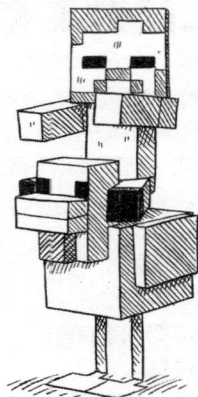

HELLO!

I must begin by congratulating you, for in your hands is one of the most powerful books in existence. The tips, tricks and hacks contained in these pages can help any Minecraft player take their gameplay to the next level. Let's get started ...

CREEPER

Tired of being blown up by a miserable green oblong? Understandable! You can keep the creepers away with these tricks.

SILENT BUT DEADLY

Creepers don't make any noise when moving, so they can easily sneak up on you. However, they do make a hissing sound when they're about to explode – that's your cue to run!

KEEP YOUR DISTANCE

Creepers only have one form of attack – blowing you up. The farther away you are, the safer you'll be. Try hitting them with arrows from afar!

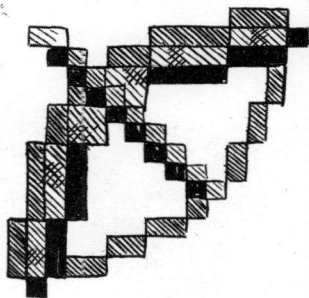

TRIGGER AN EXPLOSION

No, really! If you trigger the creeper's explosion, but manage to run outside of the blast radius in time, then you can take out the creeper without even needing a weapon!

USE CREEPERS TO ATTACK

Lots of hostile mobs on your tail? Trigger a creeper's detonation and the explosion will hurt nearby mobs, too. Just make sure YOU don't get caught in the blast!

BASIC BASES

Your first base doesn't have to be complicated, but here are some security tips to consider!

SLOW SWIM

You don't want to leave the house and walk straight into a creeper! Dig a moat around your base – as wide as you choose – and it could slow down any nearby creepers!

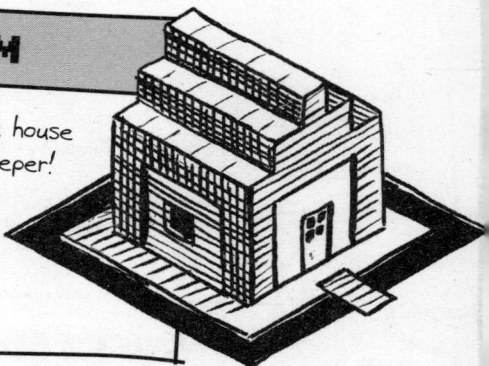

ON TOP OF THE WORLD

Picking off your enemies from a rooftop is a great way to get an advantage. Just make sure the roof can be easily accessed ... only by you!

STOCK UP

Try to fill your chests with arrows, weapons and food. It would be a disaster to be trapped inside your base unarmed and hungry!

DON'T BE A BLOCK SNOB

This is your first ever base, so build it
out of whatever you can find! A base
made of dirt blocks may look a little
basic, but prioritise things such as
security, resources and places to put
your treasure for now. Besides,
a base made of dirt is actually harder
for other players to spot. Result!

ONE WAY GLASS

This camouflaged entrance will let you safely watch for hostile mobs – and get the jump on them!

1 Dig a large cave opening in the side of a cliff, then place a crafting table and a furnace inside.

2 Mix glass with amethyst shards to craft tinted glass. You will be able to see through it, however, mobs can't.

3 Place the tinted glass across your cave opening, allowing space for a door on one side.

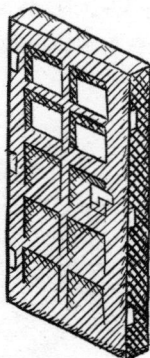

4 Craft a wooden door and place it in the space.

5 Keep watch for hostile mobs, then startle them by attacking as soon as they've passed by.

ADVANCED TIP
Place dispensers containing arrows in the walls. Use pressure plates or tripwire – and some redstone – to set them up!

11

SKELETON

If you don't want to be defeated by this miserable pile of bones, try these top skeleton-slaying tips!

FIGHT OR FLIGHT?

Skeletons can hit you with their arrows from up to 16 blocks away. So unless you can dash at least 17 blocks away, you're better off fighting than fleeing!

A CLEAR SOLUTION

Build a glass wall that's two blocks high and the skeleton will still approach you, but won't fire arrows (they'd only hit the glass anyway). That means you can watch as they move into melee combat range without hitting you. Nice!

A LESS CLEAR SOLUTION

If a skeleton starts shooting at you, take cover behind something two blocks tall. It'll give you times to discover where they are, equip your bow and return fire. Be warned, if it has steps they could scale it and fire cown on you!

OFFENSIVE DEFENCE

Equipping a shield is a smart strategy because it can deflect the skeleton's arrows. Did you know that if you're close enough, those deflected arrows will even hit the skeleton, causing it to damage itself? Try it and see!

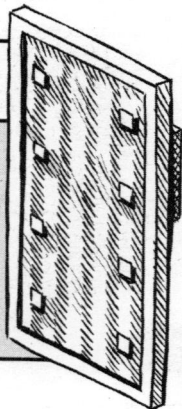

MINING

Never forget the 'mine' in Minecraft. Here are some useful mining tips to get you started!

MOVE IT OR LOSE IT

Take regular trips back to your base to deposit any resources you've gathered into a chest, so you don't lose them.

BRING THE RIGHT TOOLS

Craft durable tools before embarking on a mining expedition. Stone tools are great for early-game mining, but netherite tools are the best.

FUN IN SPADES

Pickaxes are obviously a mining must, but it's worth bringing a few shovels, too. They're far more effective for digging up dirt – something you'll uncover a lot of while mining (especially nearer the surface). Remember to use the right tool for the job!

BE ON YOUR GUARD

Weapons are important — there are lots of
spiders, skeletons and other terrifying mobs
below the surface. Take a couple of swords so
you're ready for any nasty surprises.
Some hostile mobs may also drop weapons — don't
forget to pick them up to help you in a pinch!

COMBAT

Itching for a fight, but still not sure which end of the sword to hold? Follow these hacks!

1 SNEAKY STRIKES

If you've spotted an enemy before they see you, be the one to make the first hit. This is much easier with a ranged weapon, such as a bow. Try to get several strikes in before they even know what hit them!

2 DEFENCE IS THE BEST OFFENCE

Even the best fighters get hit often, so make sure you're armoured up. The stronger your armour is, the more hits you will be able to withstand during battle.

3 BROKEN SWORD

Meters on your weapons will tell you how close they are to breaking. Pay CONSTANT attention to these. The last thing you want is to be left empty handed mid-battle!

4 EXIT STRATEGY

In the early game, good weapons are scarce but hostile mobs aren't scarce enough. Make sure you can escape if you need to. Fight hostile mobs near your house or base so you're always close to home.

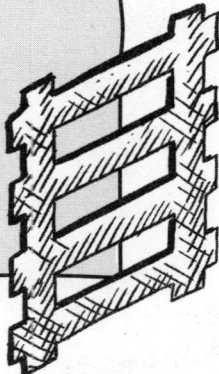

WISE WIELDER

Save your fave sword for combat and don't use it to gather wood or cobblestone – use an axe or a pickaxe!

ZOMBIE

These brain-munchers really aren't a pretty sight. Follow these strategies to help remove the 'un' from these undead mobs!

BRING THEM BACK

Dealing with a zombie villager? Here's a more compassionate solution: use a splash potion of Weakness and then a golden apple, and they'll turn back into a villager! But be warned, the process takes several minutes – during which they'll still enjoy attacking you! Note: this only works on zombie villagers that were once villagers – and will not affect regular zombies.

SHOOT FROM AFAR

Regular zombies can't use ranged weapons, but you certainly can. Use a bow or crossbow and you'll be able to hit the zombie from a distance – and they'll be too far away to hit back!

SWIFT STRIKES

Zombies are slower than you, so use that speed to your advantage. Get your sword strikes in quickly and hopefully you'll have defeated them before they can even get in a blow.

DON'T UNDERESTIMATE THE KIDS

Aren't baby zombies adorable? No, not when they're attacking you! Baby zombies are faster AND shorter, making them harder to hit. If you find one heading in your direction, try to aim lower to defeat them.

COORDINATES

Where in the Overworld are you? Find out why turning coordinates on is an exploration essential!

1 SETTINGS

When you choose your world in the main menu, select 'edit world'. Look for the 'show coordinates' option and make sure it's switched it on.

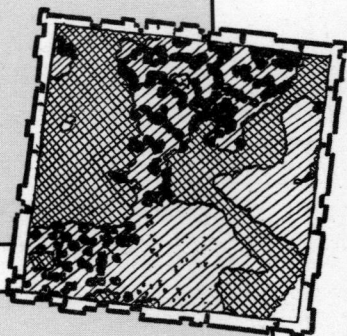

2 X, Y, Z

You'll now see your coordinates on-screen. The letters X, Y and Z relate to east to west, altitude and north to south.

3 NEVER GET LOST

Your exact location while exploring the Overworld is shown by X and Z. Found something cool while doing something else? Jot down those numbers, and you can make you're way back to that exact location whenever you want!

4 Y IS THIS USEFUL?

The middle number is the Y level. This tells you how deep you are in the Overworld. When you're mining specific resources, knowing the right Y level is hugely helpful. That's why we've included the Y level on each resource page in this book!

21

WITCH

This cackling conjurer loves using nasty spells to spoil your adventures. Get the last laugh with these witch-fighting tips!

DAIRY USEFUL

Milk is a delicious beverage and it also cures the effects that witches' potions will inflict on you, such as Poison, Weakness and Slowness.

PRETEND YOU'RE NOT IN

Witches can't open doors, but you can! If you're in a village during a raid, open a door and hide in one of the buildings. As long as you make sure to close the door behind you, you'll be safe from the witch.

DON'T USE FIRE OR WATER

Drowning a witch won't work – they could use a potion of Water Breathing. Likewise, fire attacks won't work, as the witch might drink a potion of Fire Resistance. But don't give up! Their reliance on potions is actually a weakness ...

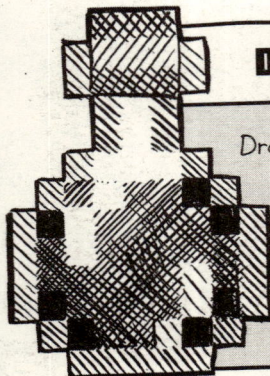

LAST ORDERS

Witches often drink potions to buff themselves. But a witch can't counter-attack when they're busy drinking, so get your hits in while they glug! Stand about 11 blocks away and they'll start drinking a potion of Swiftness – ironically, that's your cue to rush in and start attacking! Four strikes with a diamond sword should do the trick.

BREWING BASICS

It might take a bit of work to get the hang of brewing, but it opens up a whole new world of effects to explore and master.

1 OUTSTANDING

To brew potions, you'll need a brewing stand, which is crafted from 3 cobblestone blocks and a blaze rod. Cobblestone is easy to get. But sadly, the blaze rods will require you to fight blazes in the Nether. Sorry! Good luck!

2 LET'S GET AWKWARD

Most potions use an awkward potion as a base ingredient, so you'll need a lot of them! To get an awkward potion, brew a Nether wart with a water bottle (or three water bottles for three potions).

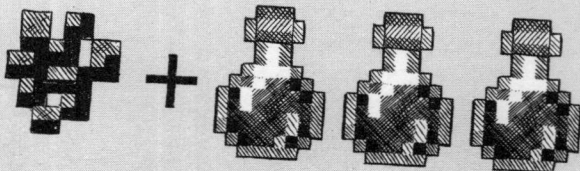

3 NETHER VISIT

To get Nether wart you'll need to visit Nether fortresses and bastion remnants. Be prepared – piglins are neutral but will turn hostile unless you're wearing something gold or if you provoke them.

4 NETHER SAY NETHER AGAIN

Fighting a blaze isn't easy, but it's significantly simpler when you have a potion of Fire Resistance. Once you have the blaze rod you need to make a brewing stand, consider returning to the Overworld and brewing a few of those potions before fighting any more blazes. Cautious adventurers tend to live longer.

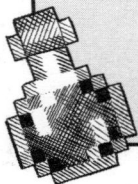

POTIONS

Here's how to brew some of the best potions. Add redstone to the mix and their effects will last longer!

LEAPING

Brew an awkward potion mixed with a rabbit's foot. You'll enjoy three minutes of higher jumping! It's an explorer's must-have and a great way to leap out of a tight spot.

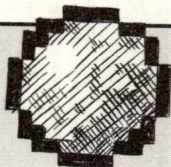

FIRE RESISTANCE

Brew an awkward potion mixed with magma cream. Lava is EVERYWHERE in Minecraft and is one of the easiest ways for you to lose everything. This potion removes one of the Overworld's (and the Nether's) greatest threats.

WATER BREATHING

Brew an awkward potion mixed with pufferfish. This delightful drink lets you spend longer exploring the Overworld's oceans. The riches you might find could pay for this potion several times over!

INVISIBILITY

Brew an awkward potion mixed with a golden carrot to create a potion of Night Vision. Brew this with a fermented spider eye to create a potion of Invisibility. This will make combat easier, but even though you may be invisible, your armour won't be!

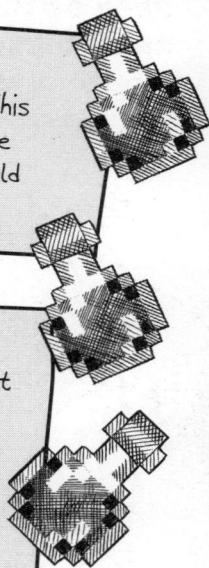

DROWNED

Anyone planning to explore oceans should heed these tricks on the drowned; an undead underwater mob, sometimes armed with a giant fork — or trident, if you want to get technical.

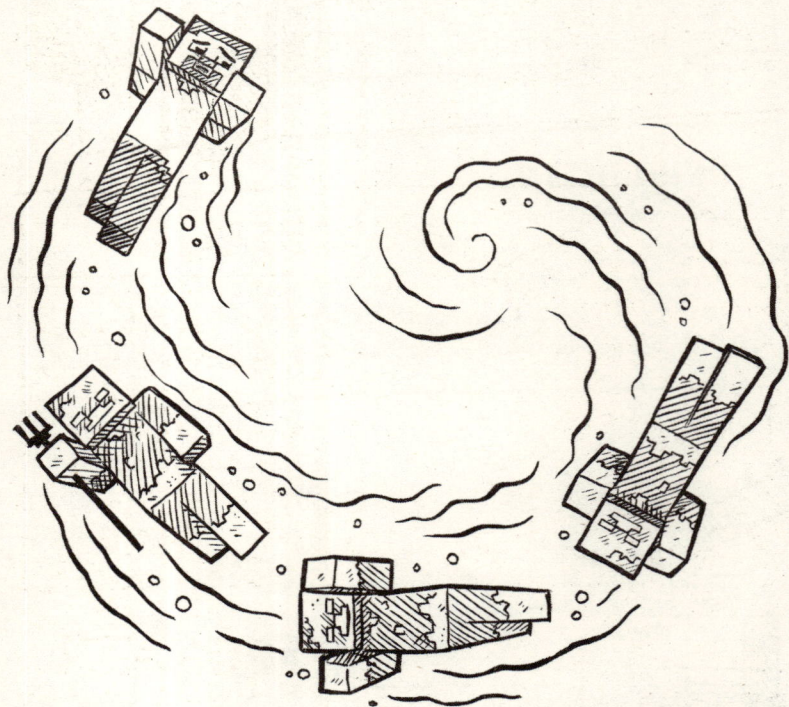

ROUND 'EM UP

Try swimming in a circle around drowned while you're attacking them. They'll keep lobbing tridents at you, but it'll be harder for them to hit you ... as long as you're moving fast enough!

LIGHTEN UP

Drowned won't spawn as long as there's enough light. Place light sources, such as sea pickles, around to stop them spawning!

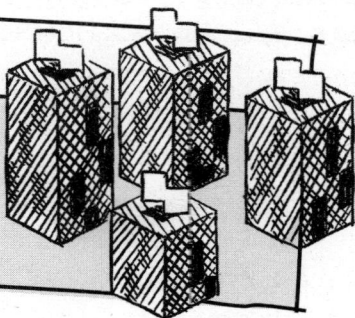

BRIGHT IDEAS

Jack o'Lanterns, sea lanterns, glowstone and sea pickles are all excellent sources of light that work underwater. This only stops drowned spawning nearby, so try not to stray too far into the darkness of the surrounding seas.

PRO TURTLE EGG TIP

Drowned love destroying sea turtle eggs. Gather some by using a tool enchanted with Silk Touch, then place them in the middle of a lava moat and they will walk straight into a fiery defeat!

CHICKEN FARM

Experience, food and an ingredient for crafting arrows — here's how to build a chicken farm.

1 You'll need four planks and two sticks to make some fences. Craft enough to create at least a 5x5 pen (but you can go as big as you want)!

2 You'll also need a gate, which requires four sticks and two planks. You only need one, but you can add more if you'd like multiple access points.

3 Consider digging a trench, a few blocks deep, inside the gate. It'll mean chickens are less likely to escape when you enter the pen! Better yet, place a block inside the pen a block away from the fence. You'll be able to jump from that block out of the pen — but the chickens won't!

4 Carry seeds and go looking for chickens! As long as you're holding seeds, the chickens will follow you. Lure them back to your new farm.

5 You need about 20 chickens. Pick up the eggs they drop, then throw them if you need more chickens (there's a one in eight chance of a thrown egg spawning a chicken). Now you've got a constant source of food, experience points and some feathery friends!

SLIME

These gooey green cubes can be a real bother, but they are well worth seeking out ...

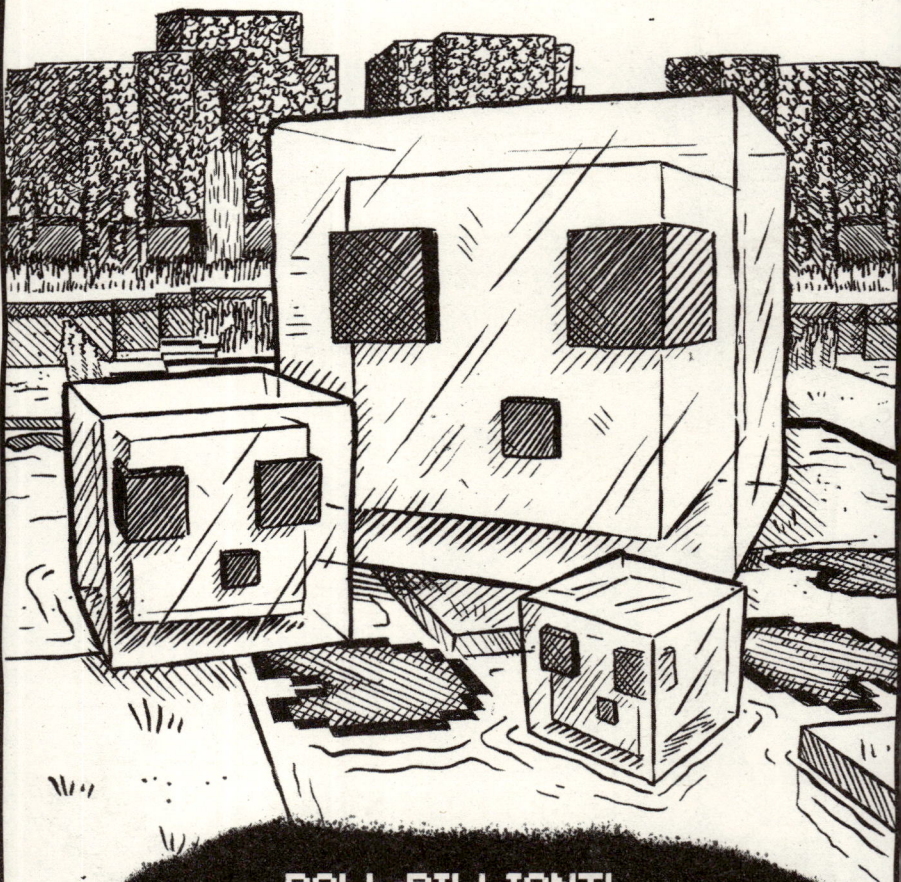

BALL-RILLIANT!

Slimes drop slimeballs. Eww? Yes, but also, excellent! Slimeballs are essential for crafting useful items, such as slime blocks, leads and sticky pistons.

SWAMP DWELLER

Overground, slimes only spawn in the rare swamp biome OR in slime chunks, which could be anywhere. They spawn at night, especially during a full moon! Although uncommon, slimes also spawn underground in caves and structures.

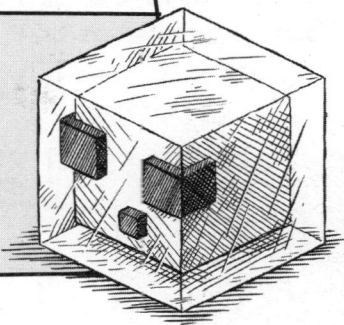

PANDAS AND WANDERING TRADERS

Sometimes, wandering traders will have slimeballs to sell. Baby pandas sometimes produce slimeballs when they sneeze ... Try not to think about that when you pick it up!

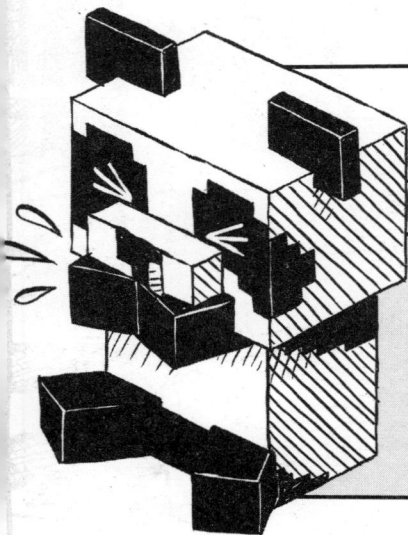

DIVIDE AND CONQUER

A few whacks with your sword will defeat a slime. But when they are defeated, they split into two smaller slimes! Keep attacking until they are tiny. The smallest slimes will attack you, but can't cause you damage!

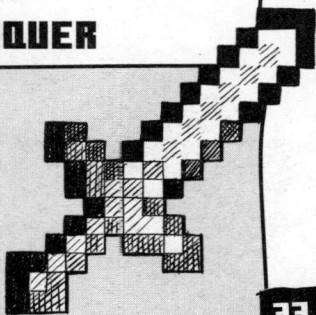

33

GOING UNDERGROUND

Chests, riches, dirt ... taking a trip underground is dark, but it can be really rewarding. Here's how to survive and make it back above ground.

TORCH THE PLACE

Light your caverns fully to prevent hostile mobs from spawning. The torches may also light up any resources high on the cave walls or ceilings. Don't dig in the dark!

HAVE AN EXIT STRATEGY

Make stairways that are easy to find and climb, and pack loads of ladders – they're a great fix for when you've accidentally dug yourself into a tight spot.

NEVER DIG STRAIGHT DOWN

Digging straight down is an easy way to fall into traps, unexpected caves or pools of lava. Always avoid digging directly above you, too – gravel could fall and suffocate you.

HEY, WHO TURNED OUT THE LIGHTS?

It's easy to lose track of time when mining underground. Try to sneak a peak at the sky before emerging from your caves, so you know if it's daytime. You don't want to fight your way back to the surface, only to find it full of hostile mobs, too!

GOLD

Whether you want to trade with piglins, or just dress as obnoxiously flashy as possible, here are some golden tips for finding gold!

RIGHT TOOLS

Use an iron pickaxe on gold ore blocks, or you won't get the raw gold inside. A diamond or netherite pickaxe will also work, but iron pickaxes are easier to obtain.

LEVEL DOWN

In most biomes, you won't find gold ore above layer Y 31 (apart from in the badlands, where it spawns higher). Sea level is Y 62, so get digging!

KNOW WHEN TO STOP

While you may start finding gold once you're below level Y 32, you will find it more commonly between levels Y-28 and Y-64. This is quite far below ground, so it might be worth saving your tools and finding a cave that gets you down there quicker.

GO HOME!

Found lots of gold? Congratulations!
Now run back to your base and deposit
it in a chest. Remember, storing your
valuables in your base always saves
you from losing it elsewhere.

WATERFALL SURFING

These cascading blocks of water are a great way of moving around caves.

1 You can swim up and down waterfalls surprisingly easily. This is great for slowly lowering yourself into a cave – whilst observing the landscape!

2 Keep some water in a bucket in your inventory. You can use it whenever you need to create your own waterfall!

3 It's easy to get lost in a cave. If you keep following the waterfall, it offers a route back AND a way to avoid getting lost!

4 As useful as waterfalls are, they are not without risk! Make sure you stay inside the water, so you don't accidentally drop out and plummet to the bottom of the cave.

5 Be prepared for where you might land – there could be hostile mobs lurking at the bottom of the falls!

VINDICATORS, EVOKERS, PILLAGERS

A trio of hostile horrors that have caused a grisly end for many adventurers. Check out these tips for dealing with them!

DON'T HIDE INSIDE

Vindicators spawn in village raids, so it can be tempting to hide in a villager's house. Don't! Vindicators can smash down wooden doors, so hiding somewhere without better defences isn't an option. You'll have to stand your ground and fight back!

QUICK AS YOU CAN!

Evokers summon vexes and you REALLY want to take out the evoker before it does that. Rush them with accurate melee strikes before they can create bigger threats that won't be as easy to survive.

STEALTH MODE

Pillagers don't take many hits to defeat, but their crossbow attacks are very powerful. Try to sneak up on them, so you can get a strike or two in before they can aim their crossbow.

USE THE VILLAGERS

Look, it's not your fault that villagers make great bait, is it? If hostile mobs are busy attacking villagers, it gives you more time to line up your ranged attacks. See, everybody wins ... in a way!

LAVA

More like lavARGHH — because that's the sound you'll make if you try to take a bath in it. Try following these tips instead.

BLOCK THE FLOW

A lavafall can make exploring tricky. Try carefully placing stone blocks in its path to divert the flow. This is especially useful if you want to mine any ore blocks that are next to lava!

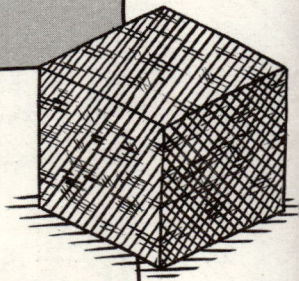

GIVE IT A WASH

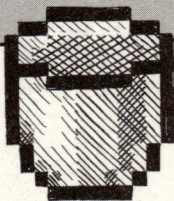

Carry several buckets of water and you can pour them on to any lava that is a lake, turning it into obsidian blocks. Great for making a safe path!

IT HURTS ENEMIES

Many hostile mobs are just as weak to lava as you are. Try luring attacking mobs near lava flows. Your attacks could knock them into it — but this works both ways, so don't stand too close!

HOT HOUSE

A moat around your home is great for dealing with unwanted intruders, but if you really want to send a fiery warning, why not fill your moat with lava? If you do take this advice, just make sure you warn your mates before inviting them over for cake!

IRON

It's one of the Overworld's most essential crafting materials. Here's how to find it!

IRON ALL AROUND

You don't actually have to journey underground to start finding iron ore. It can be found across many levels and generates commonly between levels Y 80 and Y 384.

MOUNTAINS OF IRON

Mountains are a fantastic resource for iron-seekers, as they contain tons of the stuff. It's also easy to spot iron ore in their exposed stone edges.

IRON VEINS

When you're mining between Y levels -8 and -58, you may discover an ore vein. These are massive chains of tuff blocks, containing a high number of iron ore blocks.

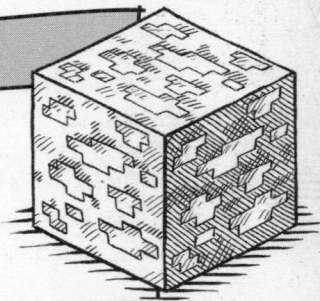

HEAL A GOLEM

Here's an underrated use for iron ingots – did you know they can be used to heal iron golems? Simply use an iron ingot on an iron golem and its cracks will be repaired. It's the least you can do after it's helped you through a raid, surely?

ENDERMAN

The mob with amazing glowing eyes. But, er, don't look into them. Just take our word for it.

SPLASH DAMAGE

Endermen take damage from water. If you're having trouble fighting one, try diving into the ocean. Or try standing somewhere surrounded by water and hitting them with arrows from a safe distance.

TAKING COVER

Get an Enderman's attention, then take cover under a platform that's 2 blocks high. Endermen won't be able to reach you, but you'll be able to attack them!

PUMPKIN VISION

If you're wearing a carved pumpkin, then we salute your brave fashion choices. More to the point, you can look at Endermen w'thout provoking them. Very helpful for getting that first strike in!

DOG HOUSE

Dig a pit and fill it with tamed wolves (make sure they're tamed!). Then, after attacking an Enderman, leap inside the pit. When the Enderman teleports inside, it'll have a bunch of angry wolves to deal with!

WOOD

An essential crafting ingredient that literally grows on trees, wood has tons of clever uses. Here are some of our favourites!

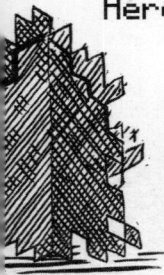

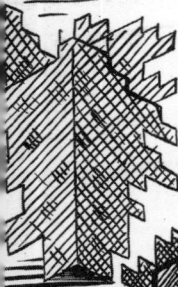

FUEL

All wood types can be used as fuel for your furnaces, blast furnaces, smokers and campfires.

CONSTANT GARDENER

Make sure to keep planting tree saplings (a common drop when you break leaves) or you can easily end up stuck with no wood at all!

BURN BABY BURN

As long as you're careful you can build all sorts of clever traps out of wood. Have a wooden bridge covering the moat outside your base and you can burn it swiftly to stop hostile mobs coming in.

AESTHETICALLY PLEASING

There are several types of wood and they all
have a different appearance . You could make
a house out of dirt, but you'll probably have
a more popular multiplayer server if you're
inviting people into a wooden home, no?

MISLEADING MOBS

Some of Minecraft's deadliest mobs don't always look dangerous ... until you get up close. Here are some misleading mobs to watch out for!

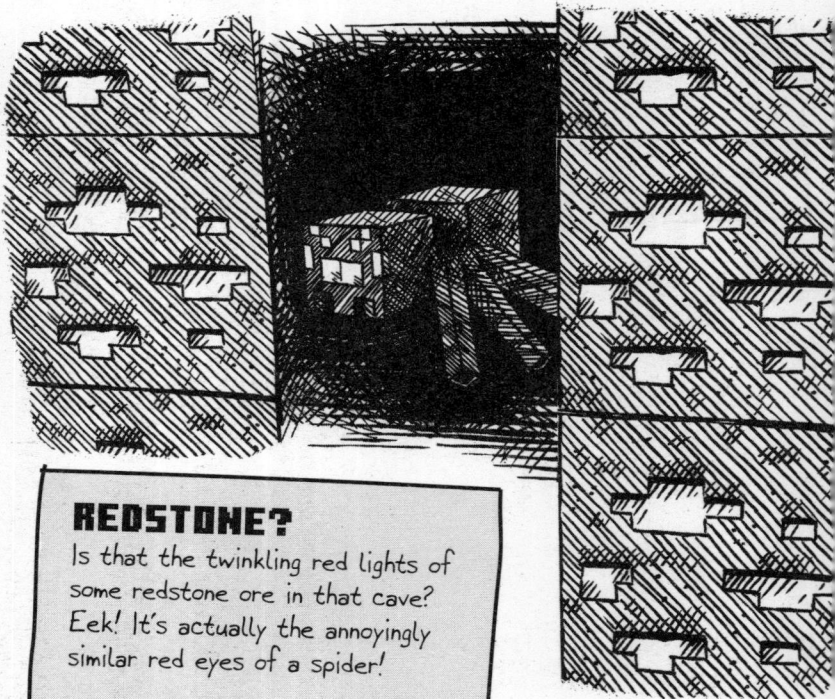

REDSTONE?

Is that the twinkling red lights of some redstone ore in that cave? Eek! It's actually the annoyingly similar red eyes of a spider!

OH, HOW CUTE!

Baby zombies might look cute from a distance – but don't be fooled! They are just as hostile as zombies, but they move faster and are harder to hit with melee and ranged attacks!

CREEPER?

Parrots are colourful birds that aren't hostile. However, this mob loves to imitate other mobs. It'll sometimes make noises that trick you into thinking creepers, spiders, or other bad news is nearby. Bad Polly!

PURPLE PRIZES?

Pretty purple particles shimmering about seem to imply something wonderful is nearby. Far from it! The Enderman may look like they're throwing purple glitter everywhere, but this neutral mob is surprisingly shy and you don't want to get caught staring at them.

COBBLESTONE GENERATOR

Sure, it's a block that can seem as common as air, but never risk running out of cobblestone with this hack we've cobbled together.

1 You'll need a bucket of water (easy) and a bucket of lava (uh oh) for this hack. Collect the latter carefully!

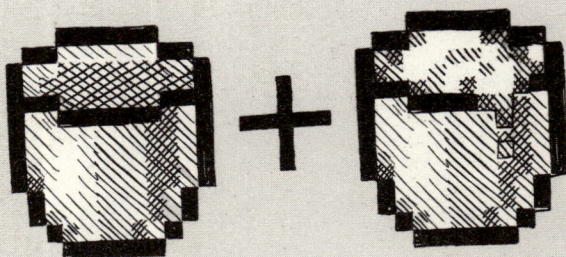

2 Dig a small pit that's four blocks across. The second space should be two blocks deep, with all the others one block deep.

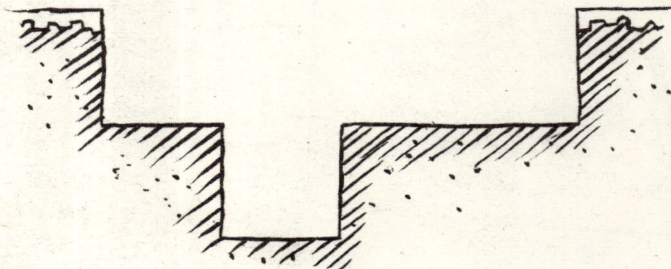

3 Pour your water bucket on one side of your pit, so the water pours down into the two-block-deep hole. The two spaces on the other side should have no water.

4 Now pour your lava bucket on the opposite side of the pit. The lava should flow into the water, creating a cobblestone block!

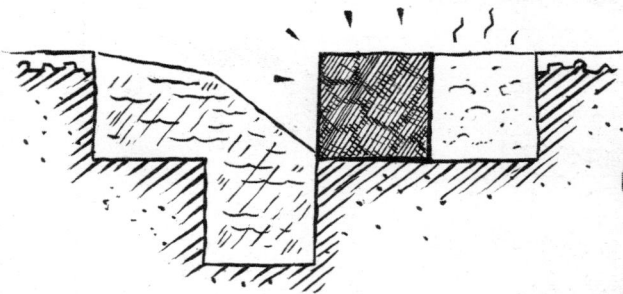

5 Mine that cobblestone block and barely a second later, a new cobblestone block will take its place. This is your infinite cobblestone generator!

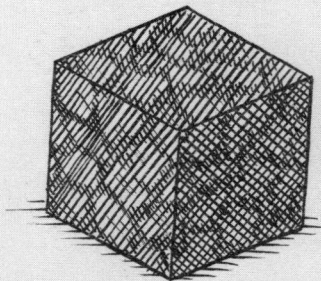

GO WITH THE FLOW

If water flows into the lava source you placed, it'll form obsidian. That's why you want an empty block between the lava and the water flow — it's when they flow into each other that you get cobblestone.

MULTIPLAYER GAMES

Speedily build your way to multiplayer success with this bridge-building hack!

BUILDING BRIDGES

Lots of Minecraft multiplayer games are set on small islands with deadly drops between them. This hack will show you how to navigate safely.

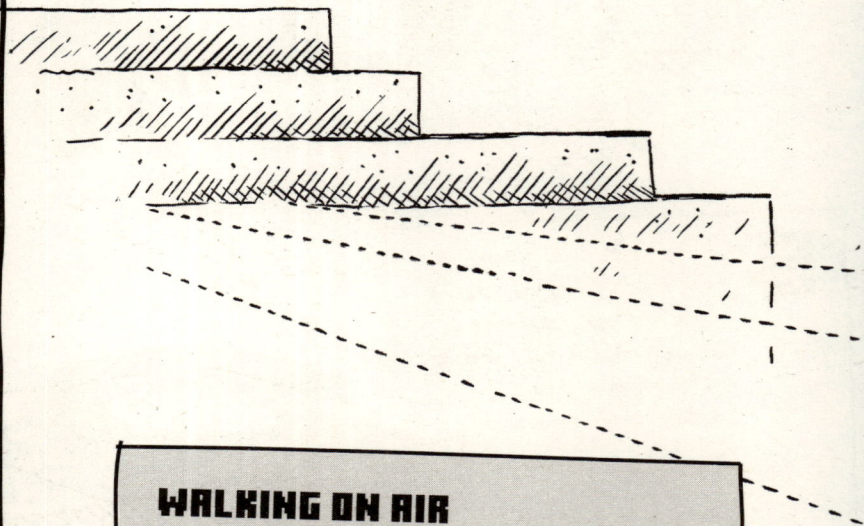

WALKING ON AIR

Walk as close to the edge as possible while facing away from the drop. Place a block beneath your feet connected to the block you're hanging off. Don't fall as you try this!

QUICK AS YOU CAN

Practise this! You want to get so swift at it that you can essentially walk through the air while building the bridge below your feet. If you find it difficult to master, crouch as you do it and you won't fall off any edges!

THE WARDEN

You seriously want to fight one of these? Wouldn't you rather fight a chicken? OK, OK, suit yourself ...

GET SOME UNLIKELY HELP

Summoning the Wither is always a risk. But you can take advantage of its incredible power by summoning it near a warden – then run away and let those two hostile horrors fight amongst themselves!

YOU'D BE MAD TO MELEE

The warden's melee attacks are incredibly powerful so it is best to avoid getting too close to it. Avoid melee combat and use ranged weapons, such as crossbows and bows.

SONIC DEFENCE

The warden's sonic boom is one of the most difficult attacks to evade. It is capable of booming through blocks and even bypassing your armour! Your only possible defence is a Resistance status effect.

SET OFF A SHRIEKER

Sculk shriekers can be used to summon a warden. Set one off from a distance by firing an arrow at a nearby sculk sensor. The warden will appear near the shrieker!

DON'T BOTHER?

The warden is ridiculously powerful and wasn't designed to be easily defeated – it's a punishment mob for those who fail to sneak through the deep dark undetected. If you want to avoid the warden altogether, try some of our deep dark tips on page 74 instead!

PILLAGER OUTPOSTS

They're essentially elaborate treehouses populated exclusively by jerks. Here's how you take them down!

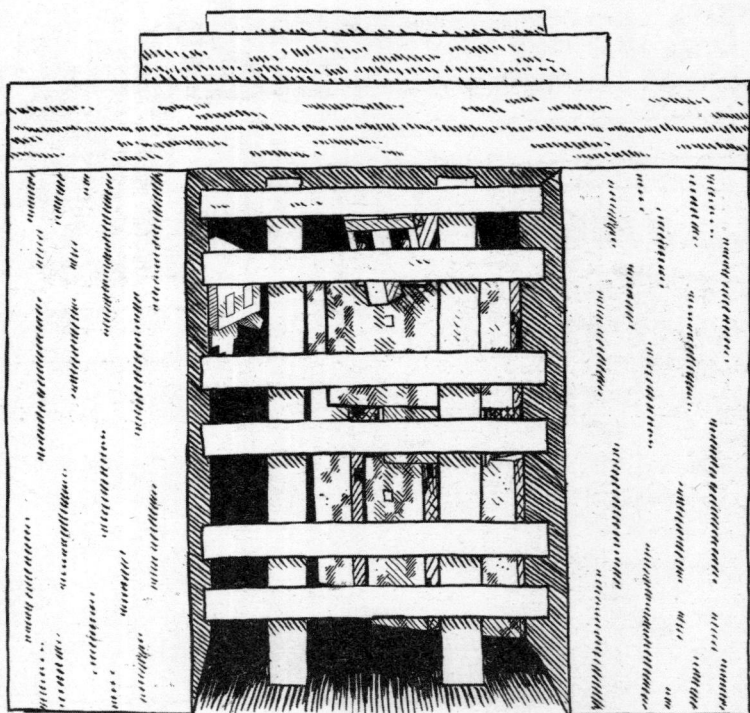

FREE THE GOLEMS

First, look for any wooden cages around the outpost. Break them open with an axe, so the iron golems and allays can escape!

TRICKS

GET HELP FROM THE GOLEMS

Stick close to the iron golem, because they do not get on with pillagers and will attack them. Great to get some iron backup.

TAKE COVER

If a pillager shoots at you, take cover behind stacks of blocks. It'll give you a few seconds to work out where they are, equip your bow and return fire or ambush them as they look for you.

TREASURE TOWER

To find some loot for your trouble, you'll want to reach the top floor of the outpost. Again, don't rush! You'll likely find a pillager captain up there and defeating it gives you a Bad Omen effect. Visit a village with this and you'll trigger a raid!

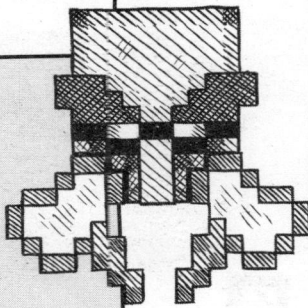

VILLAGES

Running low on health and resources? Don't mind being the worst guest ever? Here are a few handy hacks to exploit the villagers' hospitality ...

1 Find a village. They're all around the Overworld and not hard to spot – keep your eye out for their houses!

2 You can sleep in any bed you like. Even if a villager is already in the bed, they'll get booted out and replaced by you. Sweet dreams!

3 You can trade emeralds with villagers OR you can keep exploring their homes and steal from their chests and farms. Ethical? Not at all. Profitable? Very!

4 If you find emeralds in those chests, remember you can trade them with the villagers for resources! Trading villagers their own emeralds is kind of like giving them back. Right?

BAD SEEDS

Farmer villagers often plant seeds – seeds you can easily dig up and take for yourself. Sorry, villagers! We promise we almost feel bad about this!

5 If a hostile mob hits an iron golem, the golem will strike back. In fact, a golem will also target hostile mobs without being hit. Now that's what we call a free bodyguard!

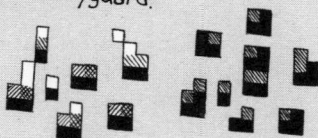

VILLAGE RAIDS

Pillagers, vindicators, witches, evokers, ravagers – oh my, that's a lot! Survive a village onslaught with these tips.

GO, GO, GOLEM!

Iron golems that are in the village will attack any hostile mobs. Don't over-rely on them (they can still perish), but they're great distractions and can help you out in combat.

KEEP YOUR DISTANCE

Ranged weapons are essential as it's easy to be overwhelmed. Try getting on top of a villager's house and picking off enemies from afar with your bow.

KNOW WHEN TO HIDE

Don't try to take on an entire wave of mobs at once! Wait for the mobs to spread out, then eliminate them one by one. If three or more are after you, run and hide!

GOLDEN APPLE

Eating golden apples might sound like a costly thing to do, but they're the perfect snack to help you survive a raid. Their effect will grant you an additional two hearts to your health bar and they also speed-up your healing time. Tasty!

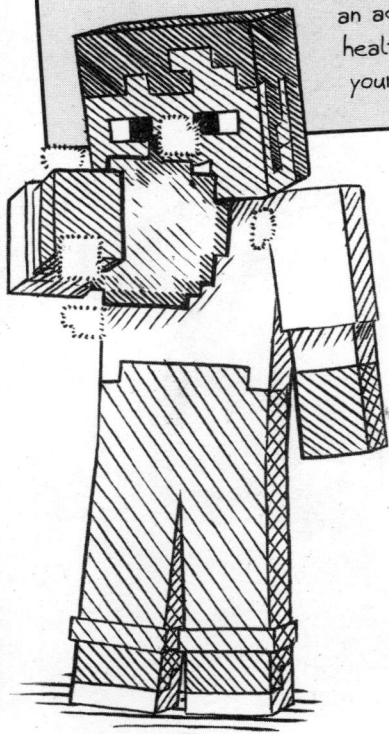

RING THE BELL

Find the bell at the village's meeting point. Ringing this will cause villagers within 32 blocks to return to their houses. Once they have, block off their doors with solid blocks and they'll be protected from most of the raiding mobs!

HORSE TAMING

Exploring the Overworld? You'll want the speed of a steed – here's how to tame one!

FIND A HORSE

Can't find a horse? Try exploring the plains biomes to find one.

HOP ABOARD!

Attempt to ride a horse and it'll soon buck you off. Don't get disheartened. Just keep trying to ride it. Feeding it an apple can speed up the process, too!

SADDLE UP

To control the horse, you'll need to equip it with a saddle. Saddles can be found in chests, traded with some villagers or even caught when you're enjoying some fishing!

COW BREEDING

Whether you want a steady supply of beef or just a delightful baby cow, here's what you need to do!

IT TAKES TWO

You'll need two cows for this tip. We'd recommend building a fence of some sort to keep them close to each other!

TASTY WHEAT

Feed the cows wheat and red
hearts will appear over them.
They'll soon turn to each other ...

CUTEST COW

The hearts will disappear and a baby
cow will appear in their place. How
cute! Now you just need to wait
eagerly for it to grow up, so it will
drop raw beef. Yum!

BASE DEFENCE SYSTEM

This effective defence system should be placed in or just outside your base. Use a fence to guide any approaching mobs to walk into its path.

1 Dig a trench, 2 blocks deep and 3 blocks wide. Place redstone dust in the middle and a piston on each side.

2 Place a dirt block above the redstone dust, and an observer on top of each piston. The arrows should face the opposite direction of where you want them to fire.

3 Place two observers at ground level, behind the arrow of the first observers. The arrows on top should be pointing in the direction you want to fire your arrows.

4 Place two dispensers in front of the two observers from step 3, in the direction their arrows were facing. Fill both dispensers with as many arrows as you can.

5 Place a stone slab staircase between the two above-ground observers and then a stone pressure plate on the ground at its bottom, between the original observers.

6 If you see any hostile mobs approaching your base, step onto the pressure plate and this build will fire waves of arrows in their direction!

HUNGER

Many peckish players have perished because they didn't keep their hunger bar nice and full. Remember, health only regenerates when you're not hungry. So try these delicious hacks!

1 Keep checking your health bar. It seems obvious, but it's easy to overlook it until it's almost empty. Remember, if it's shaking, that means it's about to deplete!

2 Your hunger is affected by something called saturation. You can't see your saturation in-game, but once it's depleted, that's when you start getting hungry.

3 This means some food SEEMS more effective than it actually is. A cake restores seven food units, but has very low saturation. That means you'll soon become hungry again!

4 All food satisifes hunger, but some have more saturation than others, such as cooked chicken and cooked porkchops, which keep you fuller for longer.

5 You can carry loads of food in one inventory slot, so take advantage of this. 64 cooked steaks will take up just one slot!

UNDERWATER

The seas are well worth exploring, but don't let them become your watery tomb!

1 POTIONS FOR OCEANS

A potion of Water Breathing is obviously essential but it's hard to see underwater, too, so also brew some potions of Night Vision.

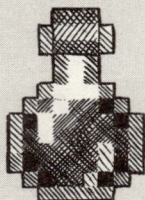

2 TURTLEY WORTH IT

Invest in a turtle shell. You'll need to breed sea turtles with seagrass. Feed the sea turtles near each other to enter them into love mode.

3 SLOW FARMS

One of the turtles will then begin swimming back to its home beach and lay eggs when it gets there. Fence the eggs off to protect from predators, then when it hatches and grows to an adult, it will drop a scute.

4 GO GREEN

You'll need five scutes to craft a turtle shell. Is it really worth all that nonsense? Yes, as sticking it on your head grants the Water Breathing status for ten seconds!

5 BRIGHT BLUE

Bring lots of light sources, such as sea lanterns and glowstones to make it easier to see underwater. They'll could also prevent hostile mobs spawning!

THE DEEP DARK

There are terrific treasures to be found in this underground biome, such as rare music discs. Just make sure you follow these tips to survive!

VERY DEEP, VERY DARK

Bring lots of light sources in your inventory or you won't be able to see much! Potions of Night Vision are well worth investing in.

WOOLLY WALKS

Placing and walking on wool blocks is a great way to explore as you don't make any sound when walking on wool. This'll make you less likely to set off any shriekers, which summon the warden!

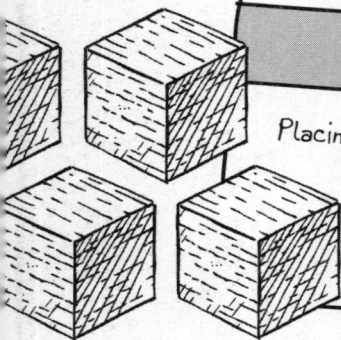

ANCIENT INDEED

The deep dark is the only place you'll find an ancient city. These structures are difficult to navigate but can reward you with some valuable loot, including the rare smithing templates for the Ward and Silence armour trims.

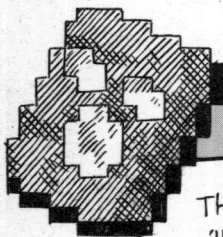

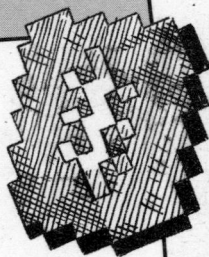

TAKE IT SLOW

Drink a potion of Slow Falling while wearing
elytra wings and you can glide around a lot
more easily. Great for filling the deep dark
with torches and light sources from the
(relative!) safety of the air.

75

BOATS

There's no finer way to travel across the seas. Here are some tips for a memorable voyage.

BUBBLE TROUBLE

Watch out for bubble columns beneath the sea. If your boat gets caught in one, it'll eventually capsize, so steer clear!

SAILOR'S EYE

Oddly, you can see what's going on in the water far better from outside the ocean than you can when swimming in it. Boats are great for this — you get a clearer view of whether there's anything worth diving in for!

TREASURE CHEST

Crafting a boat requires just five matching wood planks. You can craft the resulting boat with a chest to add a very useful portable inventory to your vehicle.

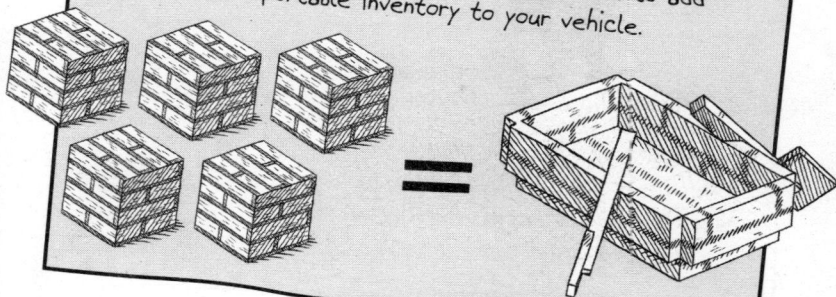

TWO BY TWO

Craft two boats and keep a spare in your hotbar. If you're capsized or worse, the last thing you want is to be stuck in the middle of the sea without a spare.

FREQUENT FISHER

Under the surface of the water are lots of food options. Don't forget to whip out your fishing rod and reel in some fish to cook and eat.

ELDER GUARDIAN

These sea monsters make ocean monuments difficult to explore. These tips will help you survive an underwater encounter!

BRING BLADES

Remember, arrows don't travel well underwater, so bring the best swords you have. A wooden sword? Nope. Diamond at least, or you could really struggle to survive.

ESSENTIAL ENCHANTMENTS

Sharpness makes your sword strikes more powerful. For a trident, using Impaling is excellent for dealing with underwater mobs. Depth Strider increases your speed underwater, which is handy because you'll need to move fast!

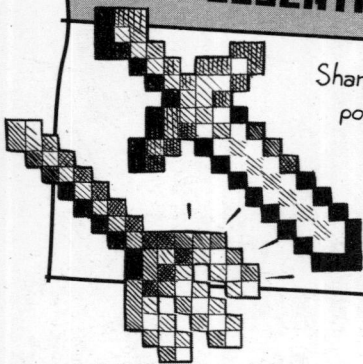

LASER PRECISION

The elder guardian's laser attack is a powerful underwater weapon! It can only fire about 14 blocks, so your best hope is to stay further away than that ... or just never encounter one.

DON'T GIVE UP!

Mining an escape route won't work!
Elder guardians cast Mining Fatigue, which
makes mining away pretty much impossible.
Drinking milk will remove the effect – but
not for long, so get moving!

PIG RIDING

Pigs are too cute to be used as food! Try making them into an adorable (and admittedly, delicious) transport option instead.

BACK IN THE SADDLE

You'll need to put a saddle on a pig to ride it. They can't be crafted, so you'll need to search in chests, go fishing, trade with a villager or grab one dropped by a strider or ravager.

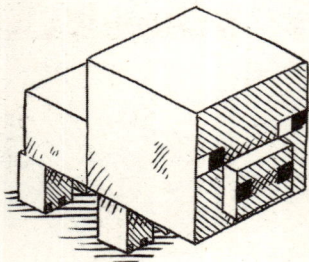

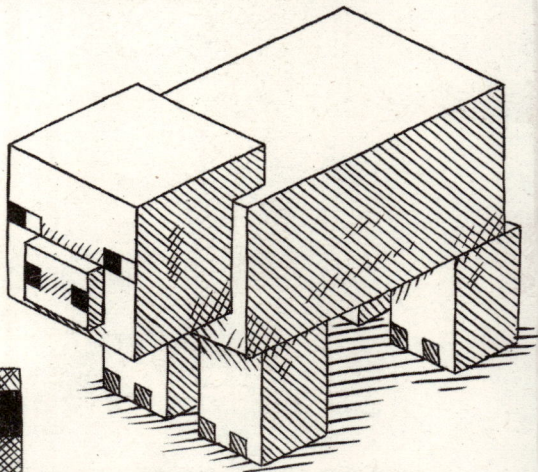

FISHY CRAFT

You'll also need a carrot on a stick to steer your pig. This is easy – just craft a fishing rod with a carrot!

FAST FOOD

Now hop aboard your pig and use the carrot on a stick to steer it! Sure, its acceleration is slow and it can only carry you slightly quicker than walking ... but it sure is fun!

ADVANCED BASES

Don't want other players stealing your loot?
Understandable! Here are a few tips for building
a well-hidden base ...

1 Build your base somewhere with uneven ground or lots of trees, such as a mountain or dark forest biome.

2 Build it as wide as you like, but not too tall – if you want more floors, dig down! This will help keep it hidden from sight.

3 Now cover the base in dirt blocks. Yes, yes, not very aesthetically pleasing — but trust us!

4 Store your loot under your floors or behind secret walls to stop any unlikely intruders from finding it easily!

5 A dirt block-covered base blends in perfectly and is much harder to find. You could even consider dirt blocks instead of a door!

SMART TRICK

As effective as this base-hiding strategy is, make sure YOU can still find it! Turn on coordinates in the settings, then make a note of them.

NETHER PORTAL

Want to take the most dangerous holiday of your life? Step inside! No, we don't want to come with you. Thanks anyway!

NETHER FINISHED?

You'll find incomplete Nether portals all around the Overworld. It'll take some time, but it is possible to finish them — as long as you have some obsidian.

BLEAK BLOCKS

You need 14 blocks of obsidian (four horizontal five vertical) to build your own portal. If you don't have enough, it will work without the four corners!

WATER SOLUTION

You can get obsidian by pouring water on a lava source block, which can often be found near an incomplete portal.

ALL MINE

Mine the obsidian blocks using a diamond pickaxe. Make sure the surrounding blocks aren't lava or they'll melt before you manage to gather them.

FIRE STARTER

Once you've finished your portal use a flint and steel on the bottom of the frame or set off a fire charge. The portal should fill with purple light. Bon voyage!

THE NETHER

Visiting Minecraft's hottest tourist destination?
Be warned: it can be too hot to survive! Make
sure you follow these survival hacks.

PACK GOLD

The piglins down in the Nether
LOVE gold. Bring some if you want
to barter with them and wear some
so they don't attack you!

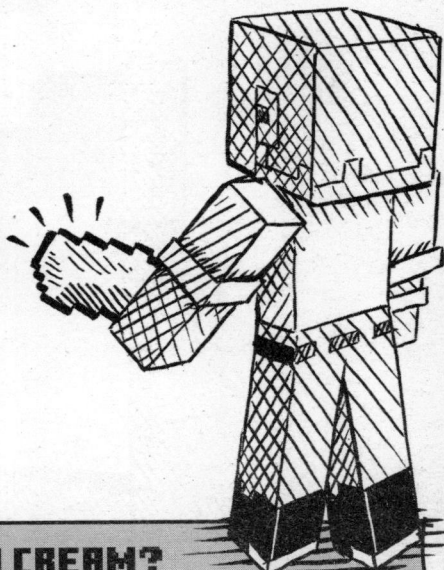

SUN CREAM?

A potion of Fire Resistance is useful. Defeat a blaze to
source blaze rods. Use these to create a brewing stand and
make blaze powder for potions to use on future visits.

YOU'LL NETHER LEAVE

That Nether portal is your ticket home – so don't lose it! Construct landmarks or leave a trail of easily-spotted blocks, so you can find your way back.

GHAST

Defeat this sobbing spirit with ease. Bonus tip: bring earplugs. This one loves to whine!

STAY AWAY

Ranged weapons make sense against a ghast. But if you're feeling brave, you could use a melee weapon to deflect their own fireballs back at them.

DRINK UP

A potion of Fire Resistance is an essential brew for fighting this fireball-throwing mob!

BLAST OFF

There's an enchantment called Blast Protection. It's great for fighting ghasts, especially when they start spitting fireballs!

EXPLOSIVE RESULTS

If you have strong blocks to take cover behind, such as cobblestone or deepslate, you could tempt a ghast to stray a bit closer to you. The explosion from its fireball attack could even result in the ghast damaging itself!

EXPERT COMBAT

Get a sharp edge on your opponents with these advanced combat tips. En garde!

EVER SO ENCHANTING

If two players have diamond swords, but only one of them has a Sharpness enchantment, you know who's already won. Invest in enchanting!

SPARE PARTS

If a weapon breaks on you mid-battle, your foe is unlikely to politely wait for you to construct a new one. If you're relying on great weapons, ALWAYS carry a spare!

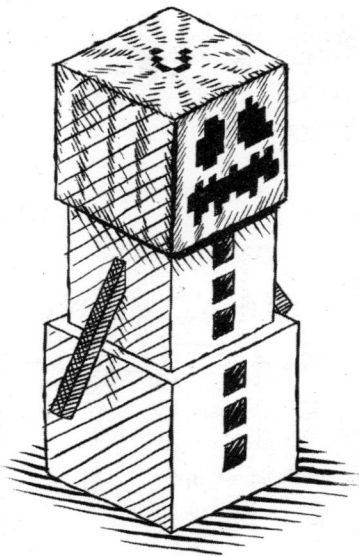

USE YOUR ENVIRONMENT

Hitting your foe will often cause them to be knocked back. Use this! Fight atop mountains, near lava, or other hazards. Just make sure you don't fall into them yourself!

FAITHFUL FRIEND

Why fight alone? Tame a wolf and you'll have a faithful furry companion that is more than willing to get into scraps for you. They will take damage, so keep an eye on their tail – if it's pointing down, they could do with some food.

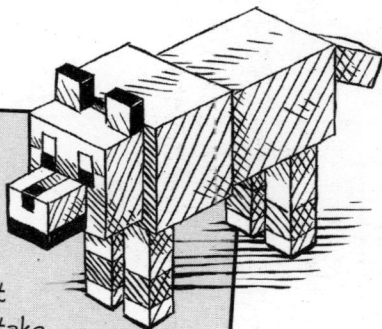

WIELD SHIELDS

Being aggressive has its advantages, but so does taking a fight slowly. Use your shield to block blows, then ready a counter-attack.

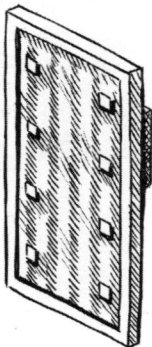

REACHING THE END

Wait, seriously? You want to go to The End? Well, OK, sure buddy, you do you. Just don't say we didn't warn you ...

BLAZING A TRAIL

You'll need blaze rods (dropped by blazes in Nether fortresses) and Ender pearls (dropped by Endermen everywhere). Both are incredibly tough to obtain, so be prepared with food and weapons!

EYE SEE WHAT TO DO

Turn your blaze rods into blaze powder and craft them with Ender pearls to get eyes of Ender. Craft as many as you can – you may need a lot of these.

EYE SPY

Throw an eye of Ender and it will float 12 blocks in the direction of the nearest stronghold. If it floats up before dropping, the stronghold is far away. If it floats downwards, the stronghold is below your position.

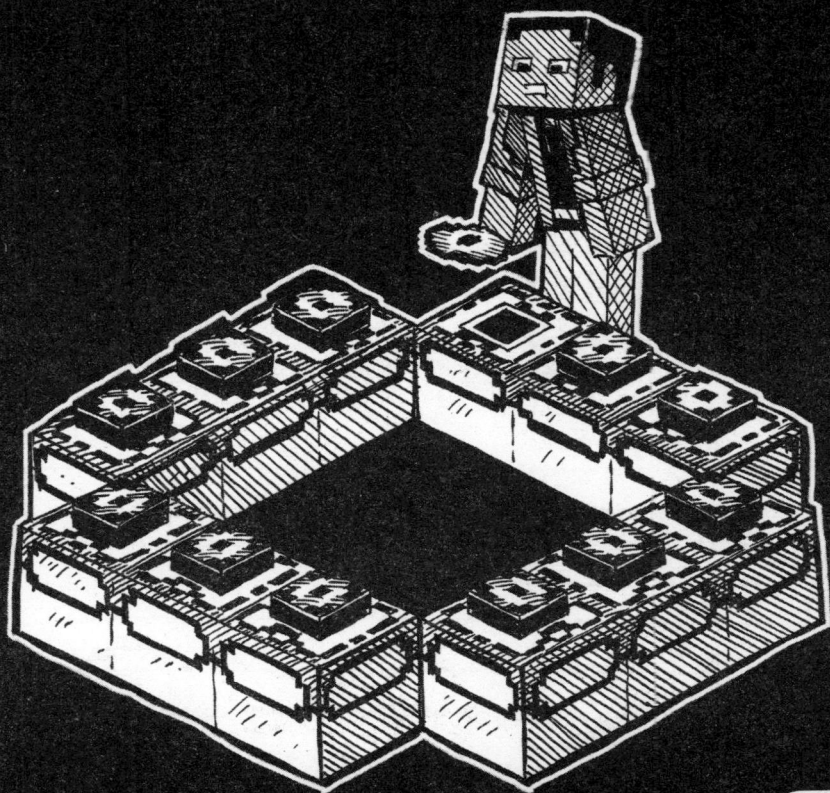

ENDER DRAGON

Defeat the Ender Dragon by throwing it a sleepover! Wait ... that can't be right. Can it?

1 Craft at least 20 yellow beds before heading into the End. Why yellow? No reason. It's just a nice colour!

2 Don't JUST bring beds though! Wear netherite armour, bring your best weapons and plenty of good food.

3 Destroy the End crystals, or the Ender Dragon's health will recharge. Some are in cages, so try to fire arrows into the cage's lower corner until you hit them!

4 Place your beds in a line, two blocks apart, on the exit portal. This is where the Ender dragon will hover throughout your battle.

5 By placing a block of obsidian between you and the beds, you will stop the explosion hitting you too. The block will take most of the damage! A potion of Blast Resistance will also help!

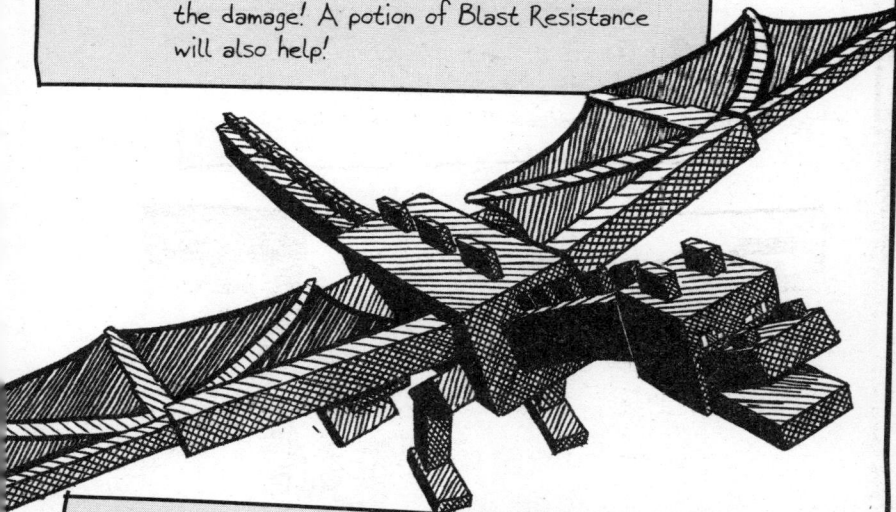

6 Provoke the Ender Dragon by firing an arrow at it. It'll become aggressive. Try not to panic!

IT'S A BLAST

Once the Ender Dragon is close enough, go to sleep in a bed to create a MASSIVE explosion! Beds explode if you try sleeping in the End – and you'll catch the dragon in the crossfire!